HEY SPOT: SPOTTED ANIMALS OF THE WORLD

Some animals have spots,
which they use to blend
into their environment.

The Dalmatian is a breed of large dog. All pups are born pure white and only begin to develop their spots around 2-3 weeks old. By the age of 4 weeks all spots will be present.

Leopards are part of the cat family. Leopards are mostly nocturnal, hunting prey at night. A leopard's tail is just about as long as its entire body.

The jaguar is the largest cat in the Americas. Their name comes from the word "yajuar." Yajuar means "he who kills with one leap."

Peafowl belong to pheasant family. Male peafowl is called peacock while female is called peahen. Beautiful and colorful tails are characteristic only for the males.

The cheetah
is the fastest
land animal
in the world.
Accelerating from
0 to 96 km/h
in three seconds.
A cheetah has
amazing eyesight
during the day
and can spot prey
from 5 km away.

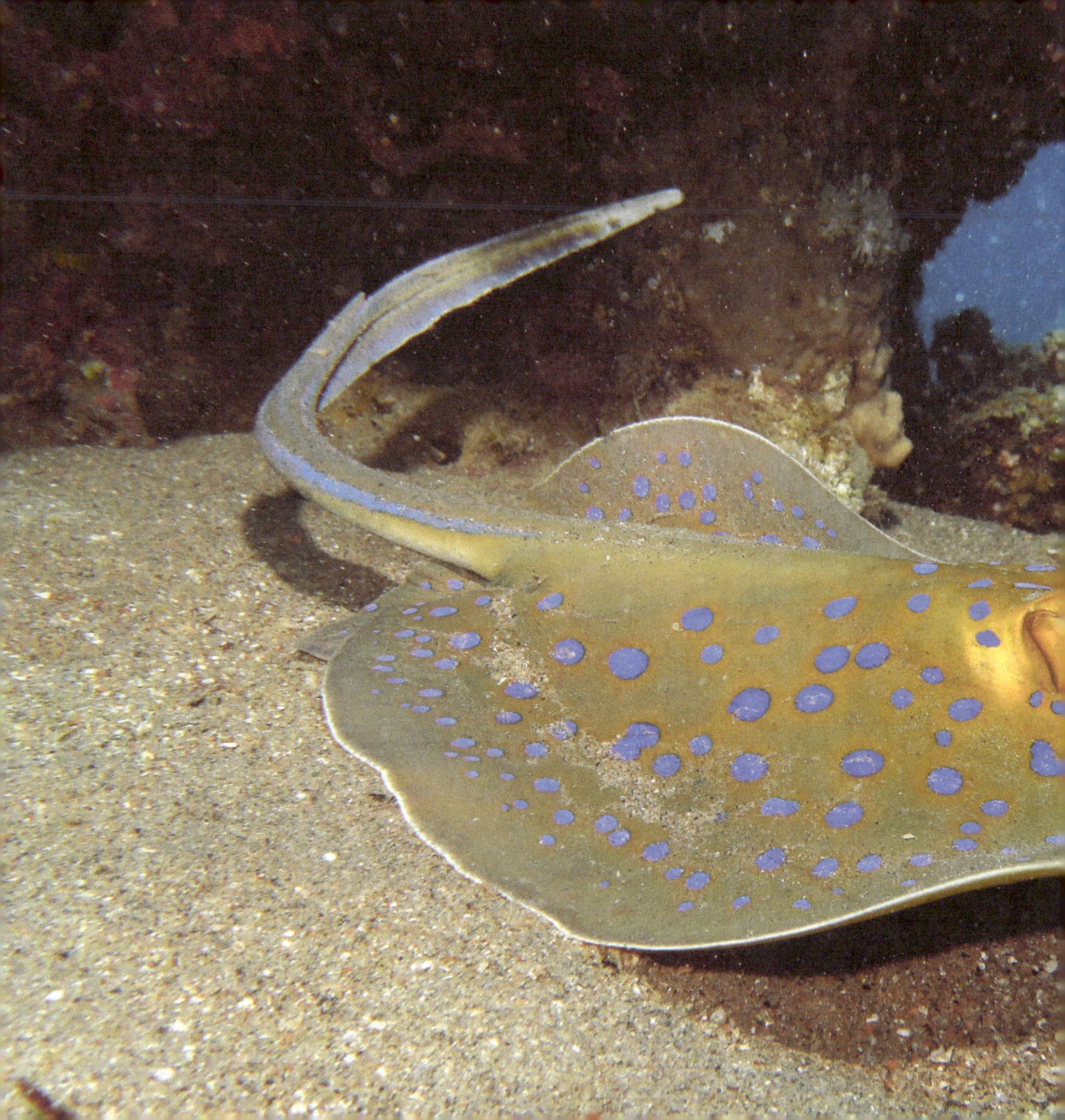

Blue spotted rays has beautiful blue spots on the top part of its body. The blue spotted ray is ovoviviparous, meaning the mother gives birth to live babies known as pups.

The spotted
salamander is
common in
the eastern
United States
and Canada.
Adult spotted
salamanders live
about 20 years
but some have
been recorded
as old as thirty.

www.ingramcontent.com/pod-product-compliance
Lightning Source LLC
Chambersburg PA
CBHW060621120726
48002CB00010B/3063